THE LITTLE BOOK OF
BIG PROFITS

*How to Make Your Money Grow
in Today's Stock Market*

WILLIAM M. BUCHSBAUM

Macmillan Spectrum
An imprint of Macmillan • USA

ISBN 0-02-861283-3

Library of Congress Cataloging Card Number: 96-070374

10 9 8 7 6 5 4 3 2 1

Interpretation of the printing code: the rightmost number of the first series of numbers is the year of the book's printing; the rightmost number of the second series of numbers is the number of the book's printing. For example, a printing code of 96-1 shows that the first printing occurred in 1996.

MarketScope Earnings Estimates reprinted by Permission of Standard & Poor's, a division of The McGraw Hill Companies.

Reprinted or quoted by permission from STOCK MARKET LOGIC, $40, published by The Institute for Econometric Research, 2200 SW 10th Street, Deerfield Beach, FL 33442; telephone 800-442-9000.

Publisher: Theresa Murtha
Managing Editor: Michael Cunningham
Development Editor: Debra Wishik Englander
Production Editor: Lori Lyons
Cover Designer: Michael Freeland
Book Design: Amy Peppler Adams, designLab, Seattle
Production Team: Holly Wittenberg, Lissa Auciello, John Ley, Angel Perez and Hilary Smith

Printed in the United States of America

To my wife Jane, who has always had confidence in me and encouraged me through life.

To my children Tony, Regie, and Allison, who have continually been my inspiration.

To my grandchildren Brian, Jonathan, and Jeremy.

To my late mother Katharine, who always kept the faith and knew I would be successful in whatever I undertook.

Acknowledgments

After 26 years in the brokerage business, I must use this occasion to acknowledge a few friends and colleagues who have helped and encouraged me and inspired me to heights I never dared imagine.

To Dick Knowlton, I offer a special thanks. Working with you over the years has been exceptional and exhilarating. To Rodney Kalil, thank you for giving me an idea a minute. To Hal Province, thanks for your trustworthiness. To Jane and Gunther Wittich, thank you for your undying support as clients, as friends, as students, and most importantly, as teachers.

I must also mention a few colleagues who helped me tremendously throughout my career: Hermie Kohlmeyer Jr., C.B. Brewster, Frank Jodoin, Van Musso, and John Lucin.

Many thanks are also due my son, Tony. Without his help creating this book, I would have been completely lost. His revisions and suggestions and encouragement were what kept me going.

To the good friends who helped me whip this book into shape, I am eternally grateful. These include Ivan Barnett, Richard Thorpe, Marcia Miller, Lara Dario, Harriet Slavich, and especially my close friend,

Professor Steve Blumberg, who did everything in his power to make this book first-class.

Finally, I must thank my agent, Laurie Harper, and my editor at Macmillan, Debby Englander, who have guided me through the daunting task of preparing this book for publication.

Bill Buchsbaum
Summer 1996
Santa Fe, NM
505-989-2748

Contents

Preface

The Little Book of Big Profits is all about the game. The investment game. Like every other game, the investment game has a set of rules. The rules tell you when to roll the dice, when to pass "go," when to collect $200, how to buy and sell properties. And, most important of all, how to win.

If you've ever invested in the stock market, you know that the rules—and the odds—are not stacked in your favor. It's up to you to turn them to your favor by learning everything you possibly can about the market, economic trends, the companies your broker recommends, and those companies you might want to recommend to your broker.

When you play what I call "the profit game," remember that the only people with a vital interest in your winning big are you and your broker. So play the game, but don't play with just your money. Play it with your brain. Play it wisely. The profit game can be fun and exciting. Remember, though, that the real point of the game is, of course, to make money. And the way to make money in the profit game is to play by rules that favor you.

Think of *The Little Book of Big Profits* as a guide. Even better, think of it as your new investment rule book.

Introduction

Few financial endeavors have occupied the efforts of more people over more years with less success than their efforts to "beat the market." So many have tried and failed that it has become popular, especially in academic circles, to believe that no one can consistently outperform the averages.

I affirm, however, that nothing can be further from the truth! Granted, everyone cannot beat the market, simply because everyone *is* the market. But that does not preclude the possibility that some investors, using more sophisticated approaches, can earn above-average returns on their investments. To be one of these elite investors, however, you must develop a logical investment strategy that takes advantage of the very weaknesses that deny superior returns to most investors.

In order to increase your stock market profits, you first must reject the concept that chance alone governs who wins and who loses on Wall Street. Most speculators who seek a "get rich quick" solution end up among the big losers. Almost without exception, investors who expect to double their money every year will fail, while those with reasonable objectives and a sophisticated and rational approach will usually be well rewarded for their efforts.

You may wonder then, based upon a rational approach toward investing, what is a reasonable return?

The answer to that question is best supplied by you and your investment advisor; "reasonable," after all, is subjective. In my own business, over a full market cycle of approximately 5 years, it has been my objective to help my clients strive for an annual compound growth rate of 20% or more, subject to economic conditions, inflation, higher interest rates, and other related factors.

In this book, I will show you how you can achieve a similar return on your investments.

CHAPTER 1

Getting a Grip on the Basics

The "stock market" is rarely taught in high school or even at the college level. Investment courses usually are selected only by students who have specialized business interests. In fact, despite the abundance of information currently available, even seasoned investors find it difficult to educate themselves. Free pamphlets and superficial guides provide little substance; encyclopedic texts are too intimidating; and the "get rich quick" books delude investors with false hopes of easy gains.

So where can you go to learn how to use stocks to your advantage? Over the years, I've learned that the only way is to seek out a qualified broker who focuses his research on companies that show a pattern of consistent internal growth.

My suggestion to those who choose to do their own research is this: you must find a place to begin, a reliable source that provides up-to-date and accurate information. Try business publications such as *Barron's*, *Investor's Business Daily*, *The Wall Street Journal*, *Business Week*, or *Forbes* (among dozens of others). You can also subscribe to monthly advisory letters, such as "The N.P.T. Review" (800-454-1345) and "O.T.C. Insights" (800-955-9566). Concentrate on the factors that move stocks, such as current revenues and earnings growth rates balanced against the comparable period of the preceding year. Information you find in the newspapers about changes in company management and a company's acquisitions is always important and is a good starting point for your research.

If you want your money to make more money—and who doesn't—you and your broker must establish an investment structure. *Structure* is as critical to the success of any investment program as it is to success in the business world and in private endeavors.

While each person has different investment objectives, everyone has one common goal: to make money. With that paramount purpose in mind, you must learn to take advantage of what I call "The Growth Stock Theory." That theory is explained in Chapter 5, but first you must learn the important basic concepts of selecting the right stocks.

CHAPTER 2

Another Day, Another 96 Cents

What is your money really worth? Not as much as you think.

Fifteen years ago, a single woman moved to an affluent part of the United States and purchased a home. She invested her remaining funds in fixed income securities (bonds) to generate an income stream that would enable her to sustain the lifestyle she was accustomed to. After 10 years she began to feel the economic pinch—that is, her income was insufficient to keep up with her cost of living. She had no hedge against inflation. Eventually, she was forced to sell her house and move elsewhere.

Investing for capital appreciation or growth in *equities* (stocks) is essential for those who expect to live another 10 years or more, because it is those people who will be subject to the loss of purchasing power due to inflation.

For example, from 1980 through 1990 inflation caused purchasing power to decline dramatically. In 1980 (see Figure 2-1), $100 bought $100 in goods and services. But in 1990, the value of those goods was only $63.49.

A little perspective: the 1990 value represents a 3.65% drop per year in purchasing power over that 10-year period.

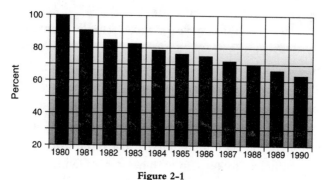

Figure 2-1
Real value of $100 over the last 10 years (based upon historical data).

If you go even farther back in time, the average annual inflation rate from 1954 to 1963 was 1.4%; from 1964 to 1973, 4.1%; from 1974 to 1983, 8.2%; and from 1984 to 1993, it was 3.7%.

It is this loss of purchasing power that you must offset. How? With careful planning and a smart investment structure.

CHAPTER 3

Put Risk on a Diet

*R*ISK—*Exposure to the chance of loss.* The risk of specific investments varies with the amount of volatility of the investment. There are risks in everything we do; the degree of risk depends on what it is we are doing and how we are doing it. The least risky to the most risky investment presents different exposures to the chance of loss.

Most people know that investing is a risky business, but even cautious investors often fail to recognize the many significant perils that threaten a portfolio. You must train yourself to be alert to the risks described here and learn how to guard against each of them while maintaining the long-term returns in your overall portfolio.

Inflation Risk

Rising prices reduce the purchasing power of any investment. An annual inflation rate of only 5% over

15 years will cut the value of $1,000 to $481. Overcautious investors who hoard all their assets in low-yielding investments, such as savings accounts and money funds, may not earn enough to outpace rising prices. In addition, rising prices erode the value of future income on investments with fixed payments—most notably, long-term bonds.

Interest Rate Risk

Rising interest rates cause investments to drop in price. For example, higher rates make yields on existing bonds less attractive, so their market value declines.

The relationship between interest rates, stock prices, and earnings works like this: when interest rates rise, stock prices tend to fall regardless of earnings growth. Once interest rates stabilize or drop, earnings become a factor again and usually drive stock prices higher.

Because higher borrowing costs cut into their net profits, individuals who invest borrowed money in margin accounts or who have floating rate debt increase their interest rate risk.

Market Risk

When general market pressures cause the value of an investment to fluctuate, it may be necessary to liquidate a given stock during a down period in the cycle. Market risk is highest for securities with above-average price volatility and lowest for stable securities such as treasury bills. It is of little consequence if you purchase securities with the intention of holding them for a long time.

Other factors, such as political developments, investor psychology, tax law changes, program trading, and even military upheavals in other countries affect market risk.

However, there is no greater risk than taking no risk at all.

CHAPTER 4

Limit One Egg per Basket

Diversification—the acquisition of a variety of assets that do not change in value at the same time. *Diversification of securities*—the purchase of securities in various companies or industries that are not related. For example, an investor would not want to invest all his or her money in high-technology companies that make only computer chips. If there becomes an oversupply of computer chips, it is quite possible that stock prices of most all computer chip companies will fall in value.

For proper diversification, it is necessary to invest in the stock of companies in varied industries, thereby reducing the ever-present risk of owning common stocks. It is also important for companies to diversify, as well, into many products that are associated with their main line business. For instance, a computer chip company must manufacture varied sizes and types of chips and perform constant research and development to keep abreast or ahead of its competition in order to not lose market share. However, to venture into other unfamiliar, nonrelated businesses is very risky. The old adage, "a jack of all trades and a master of none," is apropos to companies venturing into businesses different from their core business. This brings us to the problem of overdiversification.

Just as important as it is to diversify into 5, 10, or more stocks in unrelated industries, so, too, is it important not to overdiversify. Spreading yourself too thin by owning 30, 40, or more stocks is a deterrent. It's difficult enough to find 10 or 20 different companies that meet your objectives, let alone 30 or more.

No one can pick a winning stock every time. The only way to compensate for mistakes or situations that don't materialize (and there will always be some) is to diversify. A good rule of thumb is to make sure that no single stock represents more than 5% to 10% of your portfolio. Naturally, if you have only a small amount to invest, it will be more difficult to diversify. Even if you have $25,000 or less, you must take every precaution to pick companies with the best records and potentials—and go with 7 to 10 stocks in your portfolio. If you can make the right decisions 3 out of 4 or 4 out of 6 times, your chances of making a great deal of money increase.

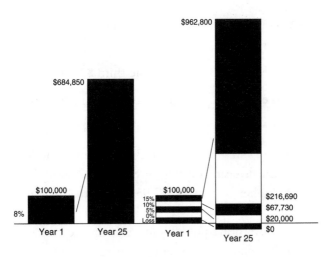

Figure 4-1
Proper diversification can increase performance.

Figure 4-1 clearly shows the power of diversification as an investment strategy.

The two bar charts on the left illustrate what would happen over 25 years if you invested $100,000 in an 8% fixed rate instrument. As you can see, the $100,000 grows to $684,850.

The two bar charts on the right illustrate the power of diversification. Imagine that you took the same $100,000 and invested it equally in five different vehicles that returned over 25 years as follows:

- You lost the first $20,000—not 20% or 50%—but you actually lost it all!

- You broke even on the second $20,000—zero return!

- You earn 5% per year on the third $20,000.

- You earn 10% per year on the fourth $20,000.

- You earn 15% per year on the fifth $20,000.

As you can see, even with the disparity in performance, the diversified strategy grew to $962,800, which is 40% higher or a full $277,950 more than the first example.

In short, don't put all your eggs in one basket—not in life, and certainly not when you invest in the stock market.

CHAPTER 5

Rome Wasn't Built in a Day

You want to make money in the stock market. You know you have to build yourself a hedge against inflation. You know there are risks. And you know you have to maintain a diverse portfolio. These are the building blocks of what I call "The Growth Stock Theory."

The Growth Stock Theory is not new. In fact, it can be traced back to the 1930s. Simply stated, this investment concept involves the purchase of shares in companies that, over time, increase earnings and dividends faster than the growth rate of the general economy. The key to success for any growth company is control—control over its destiny by financing itself internally. This means that the company retains earnings and reinvests them back into the company to finance acquisitions, research new products, and so on.

When you're purchasing real estate, one way you can pretty much guarantee success is to buy based on this mantra: *Location, Location, Location*. When you invest in growth stocks, I recommend that you buy based on *this* mantra: *Earnings, Earnings, Earnings*.

During my last 15 years out of a total of 26 in the brokerage business, I began funneling money to investment advisors who manage monies based upon clients' objectives. By analyzing each advisor's stock picks over time, I drew some conclusions of my own regarding their guidelines and parameters. Armed with a good foundation, I began to develop building blocks of my own—guidelines and parameters I knew would work for me and for my clients. In other words, I used the advisors' foundation to begin building an investment structure for the people who trust me to manage their money.

I quickly realized I could build a different structure for each client, to tailor my strategies efficiently to their individual needs—and to make it easier to find stocks poised for an increase in value.

Now, before I explain how I build an investment structure, you must understand that there are two primary ways to invest in equities (stocks). One way is to use *cyclical* stocks, and the other is to use *growth* stocks.

Cyclical stocks are shares of companies whose products are more sought-after as the economy improves and whose revenues and earnings, therefore, grow as the economy grows. (Conversely, if the economy goes into recession, the products of cyclical companies are not as much in demand, so their revenues and earnings do not continue to grow—and in fact can decline.)

On the other hand, growth companies tend to find a "niche" for themselves and grow annually, despite an "up" economy one year and a "down" or stagnant economy the next.

My advice to you is this: concentrate on growth companies whose stock prices are driven by earnings year after year. Remember, I'm talking about investing for the long term rather than the short term. This will save you brokers' commission costs, defer taxes, and allow your profits to run as long as those companies continue to grow.

The power of compounding values, which are frequently overlooked and usually underestimated, becomes evident when you invest in growth stocks. For example, a stock that grows at a compound rate of 15% per year doubles in size in 5 years, triples in 8 years, quadruples in 10 years, and grows to more than 5 times its original size in 12 years (see Figure 5-1).

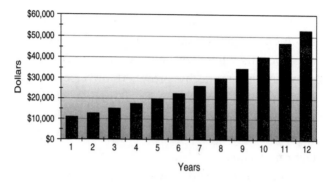

Figure 5-1
15% annual compound growth rate—$10,000 over 12 years.

The Growth Stock Theory seems simple, and in some ways it is, but it can also be quite challenging. Just remember that chance alone does not guarantee who wins or loses on Wall Street. A well-structured portfolio is essential to your financial well-being, now and in the future.

CHAPTER 6

Know the Nuts and Bolts So You Won't Get Nailed

Now you're ready for the real nuts and bolts of analyzing and picking growth stocks versus cyclical stocks. In the next several chapters, I will be analyzing the earnings growth rate of several companies. Each company was chosen on the basis of its past history. If a company has been successful year after year in increasing its earnings, it stands to reason that earnings growth should continue—*if* the company continues to do the same things that made it successful in the past.

Here's something to think about. Say that you own a professional ball club. Would you seek out mediocre players for your team? I don't think so. You would want to obtain the best players who would increase your odds of winning and would keep the odds of winning in your favor. You would hire the exceptional players:

the Michael Jordans, the Babe Ruths, the Hank Aarons, the Joe Montanas. They can win the games for you.

It's the same story in the stock market. Acquire the best companies you can to make yourself a winner in the profit game. How do you do that? By creating an investment structure utilizing effective guidelines and parameters—in much the same way that you would build a winning ball team—you can increase those all-important odds in your favor. When I look for a company as a prospective investment for my clients, I look for a company that has found a niche for itself in its industry, a company whose earnings growth rate is accelerating. Then, I analyze the company's past revenues and earnings, and how management is coping with its growing pains. I scrutinize a company's past history very closely to determine if the company fits into my guidelines and parameters. If it does, then I put the company into my "basket" of stockholdings. If the company's past history is excellent, and its standing in the industry is sustaining the potential for continued increases through astute management and demand for the company's products, then there are good indications for its continuing growth.

When you establish your portfolio, what type of growth stocks should you look for? Should you look for companies that sell at their lows for the year, or for companies that sell at their highs? My advice is this:

buy high, and your stocks will go higher! It sounds crazy, but it's true. To explain, many investors like to purchase stocks at their *lows* (price-wise), using the logic that the price can't possibly go any lower, but can go higher if the company's fortunes turn around. In other words: buy low and sell high. I prefer to look at that type of investing as "bottom fishing" for a "sleeper," using emotional thinking. My experience, on the other hand, tells me to look at the cold, hard facts of why a particular company's stock hits bottom and is selling so cheaply, compared to where its price has been previously. There's no telling when or whether this company will ever get its corporate act together sufficiently for its stock to appreciate in value. I can tell you that most investors love to "bottom fish" because of the thrill of seeing a low-cost stock rise. Much of this kind of investing is based not on facts, but on hopes and prayers.

Let's look at it another way. There is a reason why a given company's stock is making new highs day after day, week after week, month after month. The driving force is usually good news, which sends stock prices higher. In other words, higher revenues and higher earnings equate to higher stock prices. The great growth companies of the world don't sell at $20.00 one day and $100.00 the next. It's a progression of good news regarding increasing revenues and earnings that moves prices from $20.00 to $21.00, then to $22.00, $23.00, and higher.

I realize that this type of investing defies the conventional wisdom, but here's my own guidance: the most important thing to understand is that the underlying objective is to make money by playing the game by rules that favor you, not by rules that favor "the house."

⤻

Now, you're ready to analyze a growth company with present and future potential.

The following is a profile of The Enchantment Corporation (EC). Table 6.1 details each category I initially consider in determining whether or not to buy stock in a company. These factors tell me immediately whether I should go any further with my analysis.

Table 6.1   Profile of the Enchantment Corporation*

Feb	EPS	Rev (M)	Net (M)	BV/SH	Div
'95	5.68	810.6	161.9	20.55	.80
'94	4.20	598.1	119.2	14.83	.60
'93	2.97	418.2	83.4	10.22	.40
'92	2.08	290.5	58.0	7.25	.30

*Although I have assigned fictitious names to all the companies used as examples, all are actual companies, and the figures given are actual figures.

Feb simply means that this company's fiscal year ends every year on the last day of February. (Most companies' fiscal years end on December 31, the same as the calendar year, while others want to close their books during a time of the year when business has slowed due to seasonal conditions. For example, a retailer would not want to close out the year at the end of November, between Thanksgiving and Christmas, and instead closes the books during a lull period, such as January 31.)

EPS, or Earnings Per Share, are the net profits of the company divided into the amount of shares outstanding. EPS is critical because it tells you whether the company is growing in profitability. As you can see, from 1992 to 1995 EPS increased annually from $2.08 to $2.97 to $4.20 to $5.68, an annual compound growth rate of over 40% during that four-year period. Exceptional!

Rev, or revenues, are the sales of the company in millions of dollars (the *M* following Rev and Net stands for millions). In this case, they increased from $290.5 million in 1992 to $418.2 million in '93, to $598.1 million in '94, and $810.6 million in '95. This, too, is an annual compound growth rate in excess of 40%.

Net is the net income or profit in millions of dollars. When you divide the net income into the number of shares outstanding, you get EPS. Net income of this company from 1992 to 1995 increased from $58.0 million to $83.4 million, $119.2 million, then $161.9 million. The Enchantment Corporation looks great so far!

BV/SH, or Book Value Per Share, is defined as the common shareholders' value of the company on a per-share basis. It's calculated by subtracting liabilities from assets and dividing the remainder by the company's outstanding shares of stock. In this instance, the book value per share has increased from $7.25 in 1992 to $10.22 in '93, $14.83 in '94, and $20.55 in '95. Wow! This company has really moved out over the past four years, and it appears poised to continue.

DIV, or Dividend is, the amount of corporate earnings paid annually to shareholders—in this case $.30 per share in 1992, $.40 in 1993, $.60 in 1994, and $.80 in 1995.

Now let's look at the increases in The Enchantment Corporation's stock price during the same four-year period (see Table 6.2).

Table 6.2   Stock Prices

Yr	High	Low
'95	87.75	37.33
'94	53.00	33.05
'93	47.60	29.80
'92	34.10	16.85

As mentioned earlier, stock prices are driven by earnings, and these figures bear this out. EC's better than 40% growth rate in earnings and revenues resulted in its stock price highs escalating from $34.10 in 1992 to $87.75 in 1995. The stock price lows during the same period rose from $16.85 in 1992 to $37.33 in 1995. Imagine if you'd bought it at its high in 1992 of $34.10 and sold it at the mid-range of $62.00 in 1995. You would have realized an 82% return on your money. Not bad—and only because of the driving force of the earnings.

Table 6.3   Share Earnings

9 Mos Nov '95	5.48/4.08
Dec 1, '95 thru Nov 30, '95	7.08
P/E	18.5
5-Yr Growth %	+41

9 Mos Nov '95 means that in the 9 months ending in Nov '95, the earnings per share were $5.48 versus $4.08 in the same 9-month period in the preceding year. This is a healthy 34% growth rate.

Dec 1, '95 thru Nov 30, '95 indicates the earnings per share of $7.08 during the indicated 12-month period. EC still appears to be on track in their upward spiral of growth.

P/E, the price/earnings multiple (also called a price/earnings ratio), is calculated by dividing the earnings per share over the last 12 months ($7.08) into the present price of the stock ($54.37). The P/E multiple is simply a measure of the relationship between the price of the stock and its earnings per share. A high ratio of 40, 50, or more usually means that the stock may be too high in relation to earnings, or that the earnings growth rate may be accelerating. If the growth rate is accelerating, that's favorable for potentially increasing stock prices. If the P/E multiple is in fact too high, the company's stock price may decrease if the rest of the companies in the same industry are selling at a lower P/E multiple. My preference is not to buy exceptionally high P/E stocks. If the P/E is lower than the company's annual growth rate in earnings, I may consider it as a possible purchase candidate.

A low P/E of 8, 10, or 12 could indicate little or no growth potential, or might simply indicate an industry which, as a group, sells at a low P/E.

Low P/E multiples usually include companies whose earnings are stagnant, such as utility stocks, and whose debt structure remains high in relation to revenues. For example, some utility companies have long-term debt *higher* than their revenues, which is totally unacceptable in my scheme of things. My preference is for companies that have little or no long-term debt.

5-Yr Growth % indicates the 5-year growth-rate percentage. This percentage tells me whether the company is the type of company I would consider as a potential company for my portfolio. The 41% growth in The Enchantment Corporation indicates just that— EC qualifies as a company that I feel has what it takes to continue its pattern of growth.

Table 6.4   Dividends

'95	.80
'94	.60
'93	.40
'92	.30

Sometimes a company will decide to reward its shareholders by paying out a certain amount of money in the form of dividends. Suppose a company has made more earnings than it anticipated and has money left over. EC retained these earnings for internal growth and decided in 1992 to pay a per-share dividend to its shareholders of $.30 per share. As you can see, the company increased its dividend annually from $.30 in 1992 all the way up to $.80 in 1995. EC increased its dividends annually as earnings increased, because dividends come out of earnings. When companies have bad years, either they keep the dividend intact or reduce it to retain as much money as they can for operating the company (this is called retained earnings).

Table 6.5   Market Action

'95 Rng	87.75/37.37
Ave Vol	391,760
Beta	1.2
Inst Holdings	66%

'95 Rng tells me that the high and low price range of the stock in 1995 was $87.75 high and $37.37 low. This enables me to make comparisons with the prior year's figures, to see whether the price of the stock is higher or lower. It's just a guide for me as to what the stock price was during the preceding year.

Ave Vol, or average daily volume, is the number of shares traded daily. EC's stock trades 391,760 shares on average per day. An appreciable increase in volume can be either good or bad, depending on where the stock price is going when the volume is heavier. If the stock appreciates and the volume is twice normal trading, it could mean that a lot of people are accumulating the stock and it may go higher. If it goes lower on heavy volume, it means that people are selling.

Beta is a mathematical measure of the sensitivity of rates of return on a given stock, as compared with rates of return on the market as a whole. This is a measure of stock market risk—a beta of 1 equals the market. A high beta (over 1) indicates moderate or high price volatility as compared to the market as a whole. A beta over 1.5 forecasts the possibility of a 1.5% change in the return on an asset for every 1% change in the return on the market. EC has a beta of 1.2, which of course means that for every 1% the stock market moves either up or down, EC's stock will move 1.2%. That means there is more volatility in this company than in the market as a whole. Again, good news about the company tends to move the stock higher, and bad news tends to move it lower.

Inst Holdings, or institutional holdings, is the amount of stock held by institutions, as opposed to individuals. In this case, 66% of EC's stock is held by institutions such as pension plans, profit-sharing plans, or mutual funds. Institutional representation, whether it be 25%, 50%, or even 75%, is something I look for. As long as the earnings are good and improving annually (quarterly, too), then institutions will usually hold onto their positions. If an institution sells its position, it could move the stock downward.

Sometimes I will buy stock in a company with little institutional representation, in the belief that the institutions will find my gem and move the stock higher. If earnings increase and the company continues an excellent growth pattern, then there is a good possibility that institutional representation will grow, too.

There are numerous indicators that warrant watching closely, to ensure as much as you can that your money makes money for you—as much money as possible.

Table 6.6   Balance Sheet

Cur Ratio	4.16
Lt Dt (M)	-0-
Shs (M)	71.63
Report of 11/30/95	

Cur Ratio, or current ratio, is the relationship between current assets and current liabilities, calculated by dividing current liabilities into current assets. Current assets and liabilities include marketable securities, accounts receivable, accounts payable, inventories, prepaid expenses, and other items that will be converted into cash within one year. The higher the current ratio, the higher a company's liquidity (and safety).

EC's current ratio is 4.16, which means it has 4.16 times the amount of current assets as current liabilities. This is excellent and is another sign that EC is a very strong company, financially speaking.

Lt Dt (M) indicates the company's long-term debt in millions of dollars. According to my investment guidelines, the best situation is a company that has *no* debt at all, as debt simply adds to the potential problems of a company during difficult periods in the economy or a slowdown in the company's growth. As you can see, EC has no long-term debt.

Shs (M) tells you how many shares the company has sold to the public. For a company whose revenues are about $800 million, 71 million shares is not too much. To make it more palatable to those who want to own a piece of this "rock," the company may split its stock 2 for 1, and then any new purchasers would spend one half the value of the stock prior to the split. In this case, there would be 142 million shares outstanding, valued at $23.50, instead of 71 million shares valued at $47.00 per share. Splitting a stock simply doubles the number of shares (if it's a 2 for 1 split) and reduces the market value of those shares by half.

∽

To summarize, the analysis of all these terms reveals most of what you need to know in order to make a decision as to whether or not to include this particular stock in your portfolio.

Clearly, this company has created some excellent profits for my clients and is one of my big winners. To recall our earlier analogy, it possesses all the advantages that a superstar contributes to making his ball club a winner.

CHAPTER 7

The "Meat and Potatoes" of Investing

Growth stocks are appropriate for many, but not all, portfolios. Some of you may prefer to invest in fixed-income securities, namely treasury bills, bonds, and notes; corporate bonds, which are issued by corporations to finance their business; and municipal bonds, which are issued by cities, states, or counties to finance their operations and/or improvements, such as new or improved roads and buildings. Some investors—usually the elderly or those contemplating retirement, or those who feel that the stock market is too risky for them—prefer the income derived from these fixed-income investments.

Buying stocks requires patience because stocks usually possess somewhat higher market risk initially. The fact remains that growth stocks always are characterized by some degree of uncertainty as to future growth potential. But, if you know how to select and value growth stocks, they can provide excellent protection against the ever-increasing cost of living. In other words, they can give you your hedge against inflation.

Stock market investing can be an exciting pursuit for those who utilize a structure to create profits for themselves. There is no greater "high" for me than finding a company, doing the necessary research, buying that stock for my clients, and seeing the price soar to new record highs, sustained week after week for months. This is not a pipe dream; it happens more times than not, when everything falls into place.

Before looking at four-year histories of two different companies and analyzing them, I want to first introduce you to the following guidelines and parameters, which help me play by the rules that favor me and my clients:

- *Minimal or no long-term debt.*

  Corporations that have no long-term debt are better able to survive difficult times, such as downturns in the economy, downturns in business, and orders that have been delayed for corporate goods or services. In my judgment, companies that have a lot of debt simply have too much potential for trouble.

- *A current ratio of at least 2 or 3 or more to 1.*

  A company should have sufficient current assets (cash and/or cash equivalents that can be converted into cash quickly) to pay off current liabilities (short-term obligations) and have assets left over for other corporate needs. The greater the ratio, the greater the reserves to deal with unpredictable situations that may arise.

- *Current earnings at least double the P/E multiple.*

  I search for companies whose corporate earnings (per share) are growing at least twice as fast as their P/E multiple. This increases the safety factor and reduces the risk of owning common stocks. For example, if a company has a P/E ratio of 20, its earnings-per-share growth-rate must be at least 40% in the current year over the prior year.

- *Four consecutive years of increases in earnings.*

  The best possible scenario for picking a growth stock is to see four consecutive years of increases in a company's earnings per share. If a company can sustain this growth rate for a specified period, then the chances are good for continued growth into the future and also for increasing stock prices.

- *Four consecutive years of increases in revenues.*

  Again, this is the best possible indication that the company revenues and stock earnings will continue to increase annually.

- *Four consecutive years of increases in book values.*

  This is the optimum indicator that the value of the company will increase annually, both for the company and the stockholder.

- *Higher highs of stock prices over the past four years.*

  Because earnings per share, revenues, and book values increased consecutively over the last four years, it should be reflected by higher highs in the price of the stock.

- *Higher lows of stock prices over the last four years.*

  Same story here: one good thing should reflect another. Higher highs usually correlate with higher lows in stock prices annually and are signals of higher earnings growth.

Company Analysis

A careful consideration of Financial Data and Market Action (discussed in the following paragraphs) is important in making a determination as to whether or not a stock fits into our portfolio, based on our investment structure (see Tables 7.1 and 7.2). Let's dissect each component of our growth stock, The Enchantment Corporation.

This company is a leading maker of intelligent hubs and develops and manufactures Ethernet, token rings, and other networking products based on its integrated network architecture. Sales and earnings have risen sharply each year since 1986, reflecting the continuing growing and prospective demand for networking products.

Utilizing each element discussed to this point, you now can get a complete picture of The Enchantment Corporation.

Table 7.1   Financial Data

Share Earnings					
9 Mos Nov		5.48/4.08			
12/1 thru 11/30		7.08			
P/E		18.5			
5-Yr Growth %		+41			
Feb	EPS	Rev (M)	Net (M)	BV/SH	Div
'95	5.68	810.6	161.9	20.55	.80
'94	4.20	598.1	119.2	14.83	.60
'93	2.97	418.2	83.4	10.22	.40
'92	2.08	290.5	58.0	7.25	.30

The Financial Data is all-important and drives the stock prices. The Enchantment Corporation's 9-month earnings ending in November 1995 were $5.48 as compared with $4.08 during the same period in 1994. Its earnings between December 1st and November 30th (over the last 12 months) were $7.08 as compared with $5.68 in 1995. Its P/E multiple is 18.5; the 5-year growth rate is 41%, more than double the P/E multiple. EC's fiscal year closes at the end of February.

The company's earnings per share (EPS) from 1992 through 1995 increased from $2.08 to $2.97 to $4.20 and to $5.68, an excellent growth rate indeed. Along with earnings growth, the revenue growth (sales) in those years increased from $290.5 million to $418.2 million to $598.1 million to $810.6 million.

The company's net income has grown proportionally, from $58.0 million to $83.4 million to $119.2 million and to $161.9 million in 4 years; and its book value increased, in consecutive years beginning in 1992, from $7.25 to $10.22 to $14.83, and finally to $20.55 in 1995. It's no wonder this company's stock price rose from a mean of $25.00 in 1992 to over $87.75 per share during 1995. The company continues to prosper under excellent management and increased product sales. Based on growth rate alone, a stock like this one could remain indefinitely in a wise investor's portfolio, if such a pattern continues.

The dividends per share also reflect EC's growth increasing annually from $.30 to $.80 from 1992 to 1995.

Table 7.2   Stock Prices

Yr	High	Low	
'95	$87.75	$37.37	
'94	53.00	33.05	
'93	47.60	29.80	
'92	34.10	16.85	
— Bal Sheet —			
'95 Rng	$87.75/37.37	Cur ratio	4.16
Ave Vol	391,760	Lt Dt(M)	–0–
Beta	1.2	Shs(M)	71.63
Inst Holdings	66%		
Report of 11/30/95			

Stock Prices shows the 1995 price range of EC's stock at a high of $87.75 and a low of $37.37, as compared with the 1994 high and low of $53 and $33.05, respectively; a high of $47.60 and a low of $29.80 in 1993; a high of $34.10 and a low of $16.85 in 1992. If you had bought the company's stock two years ago in

1993 at its midrange of $38 (with higher highs and higher lows for four consecutive years), you would have shown a sizable profit at midyear 1995, when the stock price was about $58.00, due primarily to its growth in earnings.

The company's stock trades an average of 391,760 shares daily, and 66% of this company's stock is owned by institutions. The beta of 1.2 tells us that this company is a bit more volatile than the average market.

Its current ratio is 4.16, indicating high liquidity and excellent management.

EC has no long-term debt, which means it is able to pay its bills on time, get discounts on equipment purchases, and still have plenty of money left over for other corporate purposes. The corporation has 71.63 million shares outstanding.

If you are a more conservative investor but want growth, look for companies with patterns similar to this one. If earnings and revenue growth continue on a quarterly basis, and all so-called systems are still improving, then I would recommend keeping this stock in your portfolio. But, if quarterly results begin to deteriorate and growth slows, that is the time to replace the stock with something better suited to your requirements.

As of this point in time, EC fits all my guidelines and parameters and, in fact, has been an excellent addition to portfolios I have managed for years. The growth has continued and the stock has appreciated in value. What more can you ask for?

～

For comparison, let's look at a typical cyclical company I will call The American Cyclical Corporation, or ACC. ACC is a major corporation that offers travel and financial services within the travel services industry, which represents 72% of its business—23% of that as financial advisor, with the remainder in banking. ACC was once a large corporation that enjoyed growth from a very healthy travel card business, only to lose ground to competitors. It diversified into other areas which, in my opinion, may not have been wise. It appeared to get fat on hiring too many employees, and accumulated debt while fighting industry competition—during a period when its revenues and earnings, along with its dividends, became cyclical as the economy fluctuated.

Let's look at the last four years of ACC, so that you can make a determination based on its figures (see Table 7.3).

Table 7.3 Financial Data

	Dec	EPS	Rev (M)	Net (M)	BV/SH	Div
12 mos 1995	'95	3.11	15,842.0	1,564.0	13.10	.90
P/E 14.6	'94	2.75	14,282.0	1,413.0	12.57	.95
5-Yr Growth +35%	'93	2.92	14,172.8	1,477.8	16.81	1.00
	'92	.83	26,961.5	436.0	14.58	1.00
	'91	1.59	25,763.1	788.7	14.43	.94

As you can see, ACC's last 12 months' corporate earnings for 1995, ending December 31, were $3.11 versus $2.75 during the comparable period the year before. ACC's price/earnings ratio is 14.6, perhaps at their midrange because of its cyclical nature and also because revenues and earnings were slow or nonexistent in the recent past. ACC's 5-year growth rate of 35% is deceptive because 1990's earnings were $.69.

Note that the earnings moved up and down like a yo-yo! The earnings per share were $1.59 in 1991, dropped to $.83 in 1992, jumped dramatically in 1993 to $2.92, and then diminished to $2.75 in 1994 and rose to $3.11 in 1995. Now you see why its 5-year growth rate was so high, with 1990's $.69 factored into the equation. Without it and 1992's $.83, its growth rate would have been in the single digits.

Revenues were reduced dramatically due to the sale of one of ACC's subsidiaries, which explains the reduction from $26 billion to $14 billion. It appears that ACC took a huge write-off in 1992 from the earnings it retained over prior years in order to pay off the losses incurred by the subsidiary it sold.

Net income during the past 10 years varied from a low of $338 million to a high of $1.6 billion—ups and downs that mirror the earnings. Not much different were book values, with ups and downs during the past 4 years, and further back, too. Dividends have varied as well, from $.94 in 1991 to just $.95 in 1994 and dropping to $.90 in 1995.

Table 7.4   Market Action

Yr.	High	Low		
'95	45.12	29.00		
'94	33.12	25.00	Avg Vol	1,252,654
'93	36.62	22.37	Beta	1.1
'92	25.37	20.00	Inst Holdings	66%
'91	30.37	18.00		

With regard to Market Action, notice that stock prices, as with all factors, went up and down from 1991 through 1995, almost mirroring earnings.

Average daily volume for this sizable company is 1,252,654 shares—not much turnover of shares for a company that has 495 million shares outstanding (on the market).

Their beta is 1.1, which means that ACC's stock moves up and down pretty much in line with the market.

Institutions hold 66% of the 485 million shares outstanding. This is not too surprising because ACC is an old company, with dividends paid since 1970. About 10% of the stock is held by another company, possibly with a view to assuming control at some point down the road.

Table 7.5   Balance Sheet

Cur Ratio	.81
L/T Dt (M)	7,162
Shs (M)	495.86
Report of 12/31/95	

The company's current ratio is .81 to 1 (which, of course, means that it has more current liabilities than current assets)—probably due to the nature of its business. It is disturbing for shareholders to know that their company is not very liquid at a particular time. It's disturbing, as well, to see that this company has long-term debt of $7.1 billion, 50% of its total revenue base.

With cyclical companies being suspect in my view, I find that ACC has few redeeming features for the prospective investor. When you examine all the financial data, it is plain that the potentials are limited at best. It will remain so unless something dramatic happens to management, such as another company taking over ACC and reorganizing or otherwise stimulating the company. The price movement mirrors the financials with little movement during the recent past.

Now that you have analyzed a growth stock (The Enchantment Corporation) and a cyclical stock (The American Cyclical Corporation), let's make one last comparison to show an even more startling picture (see Table 7.6).

Table 7.6   EC Compared with ACC

The Enchantment Corporation			
	1992	*1993*	*1994*	*1995*
EPS	$2.08	$2.97	4.10	5.68
Revenues	290M	418M	598.13	810.63
Net Income	58M	83.4M	119.24	161.91
BV/SH	7.25	10.22	14.83	20.55
Div/Share	.30	.40	.60	.80
L/T Debt		—0—		

continues

Table 7.6 EC Compared with ACC (continued)

		The American Cyclical Corporation			
	1991	*1992*	*1993*	*1994*	*1995*
EPS	$1.59	$.83	$2.92	$2.75	$3.11
Revenues	25B	27B	14B	14B	15B
Net Income	788M	436M	1.4B	1.4B	1.5B
BV/SH	14.43	14.58	16.81	12.57	13.10
Div/Share	.94	1.00	1.00	.95	.90
L/T Debt		—$7.162 billion—			

↜

Let the investor beware: appreciation in stock prices in previous years (due to increased revenue and earnings) does not guarantee future growth and stock price increases. On the other hand, if you use my investment structure, I believe that your odds will be greatly improved. I analyze my clients' portfolios at least quarterly and keep only those stocks that maintain their growth rates. There will be corrections (market drops) along the way, but it certainly appears that the bull market of the mid-90's has a long way to go. As you recall, many corporations within the past few years have restructured their businesses, getting rid of past acquisitions that were unprofitable, eliminating jobs and thereby reducing expenses, and cutting every bit of excess accumulated over the years. They became more efficient by streamlining their businesses, and the end result will see an increase in corporate earnings growth over the next few years, provided their services and/or products remain in demand. With corporate earnings increasing, with interest rates trending lower, and with inflation under control, I feel we have the ingredients to be able to benefit in the stock market.

The three examples given in the above sentence stand out as some of the most important reasons to trigger higher stock prices. In addition, we are all living in a unique time in our history. With 70 million baby boomers reaching retirement age within the next 10 years, there appears to be a huge amount of money pouring into the stock market. This is because the stock market seems to be the only viable means of investing your money without tying it up for long periods of time. Say that those 70 million baby boomers invest $5 thousand annually—that equates to $350 billion a year or over $29 billion of new money invested in the stock market monthly! In my opinion, this is another very big reason the market is rising on balance and the corrections are not as drastic as some people think.

Remember that prices of growth stocks are driven by earnings, and the best time to invest is when the overall market is going up. Today, with the economy growing only slightly, due in part to the approaching $5 trillion budget deficit, we can probably expect a continued increase of stock prices.

On top of all this, supply far outweighs demand. With the endless supply of goods, it appears that inflation just might remain low through the end of this decade and beyond. It's a good bet that this scenario spells the continuation of the bull market. Corporate earnings increases across most sectors of the market could surprise a lot of investors as to the overall strength in the stock market.

Remember, increases in a company's growth must not only support the stock price, but also increase its stock price over time.

CHAPTER 8

Panning for Wall Street Gold

Y ou have the Growth Stock Theory. You have the Working Model. What you may not have is an investment advisor. And you may not want one—at least not at this moment. You might first want to play the game yourself.

Okay. How do you find the kinds of companies described in this book? The same way I do: through research.

I spend about 65-70% of my time doing research. As discussed earlier, I study newspapers such as *Investors Business Daily*, *The Wall Street Journal*, and *The New York Times*; magazines such as *Fortune*, *Money*, and *Business Week*; TV programs such as *C.N.B.C.* and *The Nightly Business Report*; annual reports from all types of companies; and all the research materials from brokerage houses that I can get my hands on. Why? Because you never know where you're going to find a gem—or a piece of information that will lead you to a gem.

I check every piece of information I gather about new companies, old companies—really, all companies—to see if they meet my guidelines and parameters.

My clients also are a source of information for me. They do their own research and frequently send me information about companies they think might qualify for my "basket of stocks."

I check every nook and cranny to find companies that show the potential to make a profit for my clients.

If you do it on your own, finding growth companies to invest in takes time and patience. For every company I choose, I reject dozens or more. Sometimes I search for weeks, only to come up empty; while at other times I find two or three companies in a week or two.

With my encouragement, my clients usually find companies on their own in newspapers, magazines, and sometimes even in annual reports of companies they already own. However, most of my clients still work full-time, and finding time to do their own research is next to impossible for them. They usually rely on me to do their homework.

For those who want to delve further into research, you should use the Internet. The Internet has quickly revolutionized the way we communicate, the way we buy and sell, the way we learn. What is the Internet? It's an interactive network, a library of text, pictures, and sound made available, usually free of charge, by companies, organizations, and individuals worldwide. For people who like doing research into the companies that represent real investment potential, it's a dream come true because the Internet is an expansive tool. Using special Internet "addresses," you can access companies all over the world, providing articles, essays, product offerings, and much, much more. Where can you find companies' Internet addresses? They are commonly listed in their advertising and annual reports. Once you're on the Net, simply enter the correct address, and within moments, you're there. By "surfing" the Internet, you'll probably learn more than you ever thought you could and maybe even come up with Wall Street Gold.

Few brokerage houses furnish information through their research departments on small growth companies to be held for the long term, so make sure your broker is very active in doing his or her research. Establishing rapport with your broker is all-important.

How do you choose a broker? Go to several brokerage houses, talk to the manager, and find out which brokers in that office do a lot of research in growth stocks and have been successful in making money for their clientele. Then, interview each broker to determine which one appeals to you. Prospects tell me all the time that they use more than one broker and are not too happy.

Find out if the broker is inclined by temperament and skill to meet your objectives by asking specific questions as to his or her goals and how he or she strategizes to beat the odds in the market. After you find a broker, see that you are educated as to exactly what they do to find the winners so you can have confidence in his or her research. Make the broker show you what sets them apart from the pack and what they do to find and follow their "gems."

Do *not* let your broker dictate to you and force you into something you are not comfortable with. Let your broker convince you with strong facts, not whims or guesswork about revenues and earnings exploding—*if* the company gets such and such a contract, for example.

Once you have chosen your broker, you can begin to invest. Try the broker out. If you have the time and want to manage your own portfolio, fine. If not, make sure your broker keeps you informed of changes and new opportunities as they arise.

If a company is not performing as anticipated, get some answers to explain the performance. Sell the stock if you feel uneasy, which will enable you to have money to invest in another stock where the potential exists to continue the upgrading of your portfolio.

One of the best ways to find companies is to read the annual and quarterly reports of good companies, such as the ones my clients own. Very often, I'll find out what companies these companies are in competition with and which ones supply them with product. The best time for you to find new investment possibilities is when quarterly earnings are released, usually from 15 to 45 days after the close of each quarter's business. This is the time to compare the last quarter's earnings with the same quarter's earnings from the previous year. Your investment advisor, if you have one, can do this daily on his or her computer.

After I find a company with potential, I go through the process outlined in this book to see if it fits into the working model (as mentioned in Chapter 7). I ask myself (as you should): Does this company have the potential for profit? You already know how to answer this question.

Will utilizing the structure of the working model reduce the ever-present risk of owning common stock? Finding companies that grow annually, thereby increasing those all-important odds that favor you, not the house, reduces that risk.

Clearly, I enjoy following leads and digging for information. Although many brokerage houses provide research, and although this type of information serves certain brokers well, I'm more comfortable doing my own research. After all, I set the guidelines so I should control the research. What's more, very often the companies I find have not yet been picked up by brokerage house research; sometimes brokerage house research finds them later, sometimes not. As I tell my clients, the waiting game is seldom the profit game.

That's why I don't wait—and neither should you.

What's Next?

When you find a company you want to invest in— that is, when you find a stock to purchase because it looks like it has some potential for growth—what do you do next? Where do you go to buy common stock? You can't exactly go down to Woolworth's looking for the common stock aisle. There are rules and regulations outlined by the Securities and Exchange Commission, and one of those rules says that only someone who is licensed and registered to trade securities can purchase stocks for you.

That rule, however, allows for some alternatives. Three, to be exact. You can go to a full-service brokerage house; to a discount broker; or to a bank that offers brokerage services.

If you call a full-service brokerage house, ask to speak with a broker who specializes in growth stocks. Ask the broker if he or she can provide additional information about your new-found gem. If the broker is familiar with the company and if he or she seems knowledgeable and a good rapport seems to be developing, then instruct him or her to purchase the shares you want. You will pay the current market price plus a commission.

The broker will ask you to sign a W9 IRS form and to furnish specific information to the brokerage house, such as your name, address, phone number, social security number, profession and place of business, marital status, years of experience in various markets, net worth, and annual income. After the order is executed, you will receive a confirmation by mail. The confirmation is like a bill, and it will tell you exactly the amount of the transaction, including all fees.

Be aware that in some cases you may be required to pay for the shares prior to the purchase, if the broker doesn't know you or about your ability to pay, and if you have not already opened an account and deposited cash and/or securities there for the brokerage house to hold for you.

Regardless, with any luck at all, you and the broker will build a relationship that proves profitable for you both. Chances for this are excellent, if you use your talents for research and the added information that a broker can provide.

As for the second two alternatives (discount brokers and banks, respectively), they basically provide one service: to act as the middleman between you and the stock market. They'll buy and sell stocks for you, but most of them do not consult or provide recommendations. In actuality, they are not advisors, but order takers, and therefore their commissions and fees will be lower.

My recommendation to you is this: get yourself an investment advisor at one of the major brokerage houses. As a layman, you need as much information as you can get. You're not a broker, and therefore there are things you simply might not know—or learn—about the business of buying and selling securities. You won't have the resources that a full service broker will. So find one, work with him or her, and build a portfolio of promising growth stocks that will be the envy of all your advisor's other clients and your friends.

The truism that "you get what you pay for" really is true. Pay your broker the commissions he or she has earned, and do it with a smile. The information and services you get in exchange will manifestly influence your potential for winning—and perhaps winning big—when you play the profit game.

CHAPTER 9

Learning by Example

I f growth stocks are appropriate for you, this chapter will be of great interest. As I have said, looking for stocks to invest in is an arduous task, but one that can be extremely rewarding.

Utilizing the guidelines and parameters outlined earlier, let's look at companies that have not only been beneficial for my clients in the past, but that have remained strong participants in the portfolios I manage.

Let's look first at The Technology Company (TC). They manufacture cryogenic refrigeration equipment used to prevent contamination of semiconductors and semiconductor parts and equipment. This company presently has a worldwide market share of 70% to 80%. Talk about no competition! Here's a company that virtually stands alone in its field, and the figures bear this out (see Table 9.1).

Table 9.1   TC Profile

| | *Stock Prices* | | | | *Revs* | *Net Income* | *BV/* | |
	High	*Low*	*EPS*	*(M)*	*(M)*	*SH*	*Div*
1995	$55.75	$14.75	$2.10	$123.6	$20.9	$4.63	1.00
1994	$19.00	$ 6.75	$1.08	$ 86.7	$10.6	$3.55	.58
1993	$ 8.68	$ 4.18	$ .51	$ 63.8	$ 4.9	$2.63	.44
1992	$ 7.75	$ 3.75	$ .30	$ 50.8	$ 2.8	$2.29	.19

TC's management has done a superior job of keeping costs down while revenues increase. Here's how the figures break down. Their earnings per share in 1992, '93, '94, and '95 were $.30, $.51, $1.08, and $2.10, respectively. Their revenues for those years increased from $50.8 million to $63.8 million to $86.7 million and to $123.6 million in 1995. Net income per share rose from $2.8 million to $4.9 million to $10.6 million and to $20.9 million in 1995. Book value per share rose, as well, from $2.29 to $2.63 to $3.55 and to $4.63. The combination of all these figures drove their stock price highs from $7.75 to $8.68 to $19.00 to $55.75, while the lows were $3.75, $4.18, $6.75 and $14.75, respectively, for the years 1992 through 1995.

With no long-term debt, a current ratio of 3.12, and dividend increases yearly from $.19 in 1992 to a current $1.00, it appears that The Technology Company's stock is destined to go higher if the company remains a major presence in cryogenic technology. Institutions control 53% of the 9.6 million shares outstanding. Finally, the P/E ratio is 14.6.

With an annual compound growth rate over the last few years in excess of 80%, this company meets all my guidelines and parameters. My intuition tells me that the stock can appreciate a great deal more in the next few years if they can maintain their dominance in their industry.

⤾

The Laser Corporation (see Table 9.2) has been a winner and appears to be poised for continued growth, a growth rate no less than spectacular. It makes lasers for industrial, medical, and science applications.

Table 9.2   The Laser Corporation Profile

| | *Stock Prices* | | | *Revs* | *Net Income* | *BV/* |
	High	*Low*	*EPS*	*(M)*	*(M)*	*SH*
1995	$44.50	$16.50	$1.75	$285.5	$19.3	$13.90
1994	$27.50	$11.50	$1.11	$215.3	$11.4	$12.43
1993	$20.25	$10.25	$ .49	$196.8	$ 4.9	$11.32
1992	$16.50	$ 7.75	$ .28	$115.4	$ 2.6	$10.31

The Laser Corporation's EPS increased from $.28 in 1992 to $.49 in 1993 to $1.11 in 1994 and to $1.75

in 1995. Even with the P/E ratio of 22, the Laser Corp's EPS grew by more than 57% in 1995, certainly meeting my parameter of earnings per share growing twice as fast as its P/E multiple. Furthermore, revenues grew from $115.4 million in 1992 to $196.8 million in 1993, $215.3 million in 1994, and $285.5 million in 1995. Net income did much the same, with increases from $2.6 million to $4.9 million to $11.4 million, and to $19.3 million in 1995. The book value per share followed suit over these years: $10.31, $11.32, $12.43, and grew to $13.90 in 1995.

The $5 million of long-term debt for this company is not a factor. Institutional holdings represent 57% of a total of 10,950,000 shares outstanding. Can you imagine where the stock has gone during this period? Correct! Their highs during the years of 1992 through 1995 were $16.50, $20.25, $27.50, and up to $44.50 in 1995.

The Laser Corporation seems to be like a certain battery product: it keeps going and going and going!

⌐

The Wafer Corporation (see Table 9.3) makes wafer-processing equipment used in fabrication of integrated circuits. Its product focus is on etch-and-deposition processes.

Table 9.3   The Wafer Corporation Profile

| | Stock Prices | | | Revs | Net Income | BV/ |
	High	Low	EPS	(M)	(M)	SH
1995	$73.37	$35.25	$3.27	$810.5	$89.2	$14.49
1994	$47.75	$22.75	$1.55	$493.7	$37.7	$ 7.23
1993	$36.75	$12.91	$ .79	$265.0	$18.9	$ 5.23
1992	$14.33	$ 6.91	$ .49	$165.6	$ 9.9	$ 4.42
1991	$ 9.16	$ 2.58	$ .33	$138.0	$ 6.0	$ 3.44

The Wafer Corporation's fiscal 1995 EPS were up 110% from $1.55 to $3.27on an increase in revenues of 64%. Selling at a P/E ratio of 12, it certainly meets those guidelines of the earnings being more than double the price earnings multiple. From 1991 through 1995, WC's stock price highs have escalated annually from $9.16 to $14.33 to $36.75 to $47.75, and finally to $73.37 in 1995. Why? You guessed it. EPS rose from $.33 in 1991 to $.49 in 1992, and from $.79 in 1993 to a dramatic $1.55 in 1994, and even more dramatically to $3.27 in 1995.

The Wafer Corporation appears to be headed for another *big* record year. Although they have $80 million of long-term debt, management has handled the company's growth well. They have 26.8 million shares outstanding, and institutions control a whopping 87%.

However, if the market sags too much (say, 15%) I'll possibly sell the shares. If the institutions begin selling, I don't want my clients caught in a mad rush to get out. But it's been, and could continue to be, a good ride.

～

Let's look at another stock that has been a winner for me over the past year—The Sportswear Co. (see Table 9.4). The Sportswear Co. designs and markets, through its units around the world, men's and boy's sportswear. They sell their products in the U.S., Canada, Japan, Central and South America.

Table 9.4   The Sportswear Company Profile

| | Stock Prices | | | Revs | Net Income | BV/ |
	High	Low	EPS	(M)	(M)	SH
1996*	$56.62	$32.62	$1.17	$352.0	$43.6	—
1995	$47.37	$18.50	$1.12	$321.0	$40.7	$5.93
1994	$22.75	$14.75	$.77	$227.2	$25.3	$4.66
1993	$17.00	$9.50	$.55	$138.6	$14.6	$2.29
1992	$13.50	$7.50	$.40	$107.0	$9.1	$1.84

* for the 9 months from April 1 to December 31, 1995 (fiscal 1996)

The Sportswear Co. has been capable of competing with its competitors in this industry for years. It posted earnings per share increases from 1992 through

1995 of $.40 to $.55 to $.77 to $1.12 in 1995, and to $1.17 for the first 9 months in 1996—an impressive compound growth rate of 38.4%. Revenues also have jumped, from $107.0 million to $138.6 million to $227.2 million, and up to $321.0 million in 1995. For the first nine months of their 1996 fiscal year, earnings grew to $1.17 as compared to the comparable period of 1995 of $.78, a 50% increase. Net income continues to show this company's outstanding growth rising from $9.1 million in 1992 to $14.6 million in 1993 to $25.3 million in 1994, and to $40.7 million in 1995.

If you guessed that with earnings, revenues, and net income accelerating stock prices would do likewise, you'd be right. The stock price highs were $13.50 in 1992, to $17.00 and $22.75 in 1993 and 1994 respectively, and finally to $47.37 in 1995. Their higher lows were $7.50 in 1992, $9.50 in 1993, $14.75 in 1994, and $18.50 in 1995. So far in 1996, the price range between its highs and lows has been $56.62 and $32.62. Because this is a British Virgin Islands corporation, no institutional holdings are so noted, but I would assume that there is some representation. Their P/E ratio of 23.5 is a bit high, but because their growth rate has been so impressive, I feel the stock can trend higher. The Sportswear Co. currently has 36 million shares outstanding and, on average, 310,000 shares trade daily and currently pays no dividends.

With prospects for continued expansion with the addition of new retail outlets, this company seems poised to continue to far outpace the rate of inflation, which is what growth stocks are all about. You have created a hedge against inflation and have seen excellent potential growth.

‿

The Pulmonary Corporation (see Table 9.5) is a provider of oxygen and other respiratory therapy services to patients in their homes. It has 205 centers in 35 states. The company has had strong growth through acquisitions, and the trend in the health care industry appears to be continuing.

Table 9.5   The Pulmonary Corporation Profile

| | Stock Prices | | EPS | Revs (M) | Net Income (M) | BV/ SH |
	High	Low				
1995	$35.25	$21.00	$1.79	$274.8	$51.0	$3.17
1994	$29.00	$18.75	$1.34	$201.1	$37.9	$2.86
1993	$25.50	$ 8.43	$1.01	$154.5	$28.2	$2.51
1992	$15.25	$ 6.37	$ .64	$117.4	$16.1	$2.04

TPC.'s earnings per share have shown excellent growth in the past four years rising from $.64 in 1992 to $1.01 in 1993 to $1.34 in 1994 and to $1.79 in 1995, a growth rate of over 32% annually. Revenues, too, increased from $117.4 million to $154.5 million to $201.1 million and to $274.8 million during the same years. Net income rose from $16.1 million in 1992, to $28.2 million in 1993, to $37.9 million in 1994, and to $51.0 million in 1995.

The Pulmonary Corporation has a very small debt of $6 million and a current ratio of 1.81. Institutional holdings represent 75% of their outstanding 27,000,000 shares with no dividends being paid. Stock prices were driven by earnings from a high of $15.25 in 1992 to $25.50 in 1993, were up to $29.00 in 1994, and rose to $35.25 in 1995. Lows ranged from $6.37 in 1992 to $8.43 in 1993, to $18.75 in 1994, and to $21.00 in 1995. Their P/E ratio as of the end of 1995 was at 15.1, and their earnings growth rate over the last year surpassed 34%.

It appears that The Pulmonary Corporation possesses the potential for additional growth internally, creating a good potential for stock price increases.

∽

The TV Camera Company (see Table 9.6) makes TV cameras and equipment, metal detectors, semiconductor testing apparatus, and microwave products. This company has demonstrated that it can be really competitive and productive in its industry.

Table 9.6   The TV Camera Company Profile

| | Stock Prices | | | Revs | Net Income | BV/ | |
	High	Low	EPS	(M)	(M)	SH	Div
1995	$36.50	$21.75	$3.20	$140.3	$14.3	$10.76	.28
1994	$27.75	$15.25	$2.30	$102.7	$10.1	$ 9.50	.23
1993	$22.50	$ 6.56	$1.63	$ 75.2	$ 6.8	$ 8.22	.19
1992	$ 7.06	$ 4.81	$ .85	$ 54.9	$ 3.4	$ 6.77	.17
1991	$ 6.43	$ 4.50	$ .65	$ 48.3	$ 2.6	$ 6.23	.16

The TV Camera Company's EPS growth rate percentage over the past 5 years has been 38%: EPS growing from $.65 in 1991 to $.85 in 1992, $1.63 in 1993, $2.30 in 1994, and to $3.20 in 1995.

Revenues have kept pace, growing from $48.3 million in 1991, to $54.9 million in 1992, to $75.2 million in 1993, to $102.7 million in 1994, and to $140.3 in 1995. All this time, their net income followed suit: $2.6 million in 1991, $3.4 million in 1992, $6.8 million in 1993, $10.1 million in 1994, and to $14.3 million in 1995. Naturally, their book value per share expanded as well, from $6.23 to $6.77 to $8.22, to $9.50 in 1994, and to $10.76 in 1995. Their P/E ratio of 13.7 was far less than half their earnings growth rate of 38%, so this, too, meets all my guidelines and parameters.

Institutions hold 43% of the 4.38 million shares outstanding. Long-term debt is an insignificant $4 million, and their current ratio is an acceptable 3.07. The TV Camera Company also pays a dividend of $.28 annually, increasing every year. Stock prices did what all good growth companies do. They escalated from 1991 highs of $6.43 to $7.06 in 1992, from $22.50 in 1993 to $27.75 in 1994, and to $36.50 in 1995. Higher lows also were visible over the last four years.

↬

What have you learned from our study of these companies? In a nutshell: If you look, you'll find the right stock for you. What's more, you'll find more than you want. You'll accomplish one of the goals of this book—you will diversify.

As you can see, all the companies analyzed in this chapter would be good choices for a structured port-folio, one which has the potentials that favor you—not the house. Using my guidelines and parameters, you can improve your odds to be more successful than you ever have been before. Go for it!

CHAPTER 10

When Opportunity Knocks, Don't Knock It

From time to time, opportunities called *special situations* come along. A special situation is a currently undervalued stock that can suddenly increase in value because of potentially favorable circumstances. If a company that is not doing well finds a way to correct some of its problems, it can turn its situation around.

Look at The Computer Company, one of the leading companies in the computer world (see Table 10.1). It sells franchises and stocks them with its products.

Table 10.1 The Computer Company Profile

	Stock Prices			Revs	Net Income	BV/
	High	Low	EPS	(M)	(M)	SH
1995	$43.00	$16.50	$1.73	$1,500.0	$5.3	$10.73
1994	$15.75	$ 5.75	$ .95	$1,016.9	$4.6	$ 9.48
1993	$15.25	$ 5.75	$ .75	$ 787.1	$3.2	$ 7.29
1992	$18.50	$ 6.25	$1.46	$ 622.4	$6.4	$ 6.42
1991	$10.62	$ 6.12	$ .96	$ 363.9	$4.2	$ 5.49

This company has some redeeming features:

- It has virtually no long-term debt.

- It has tripled its revenues in four years.

- Its book value has almost doubled in four years.

Even so, its earnings have been stagnant for two years. Why? TCC's profit margin, derived from increased revenues and lower expenses, is well below industry averages. This indicates a problem with management. When I investigated to find out what the problem was, I found that the company had hired a new chief financial officer who had been instrumental in the success of another company, his previous employer. This CFO insisted on receiving incentive stock options, which permit an employee to buy shares of the employer's stock at a predetermined price. The better the company operates, the greater the profit the employee realizes when he exercises his option.

Earnings for 1994 were estimated to be $.95, but for the 9 months ending in December 1994, the actual earnings were $1.15. In other words, the actual 9-month earnings were $.20 more than estimates for the entire year!

Now that excited me, because it meant the company was going to do better as of the end of their fiscal year than was predicted. Remember: stock prices are driven by earnings.

Because I saw the potential of the company, I began recommending TCC's stock to some of my clients between $9 to $11 per share. Nine months later, due to the growth in earnings, this stock was between $20 and $22. New estimates for the full year's earnings were $1.64. With the P/E multiple of 22, I felt the company was in fact being turned around by the new CFO. So I recommended it to the rest of my clients who were looking for capital appreciation or growth in their portfolios—fast. And when TCC announced full-year earnings of $1.73 ($.09 higher than estimates) and revenues of $1.5 billion (50% higher than 1992), the stock price jumped to $43.

The lesson? Some information was evident, while other information was hidden. You could find out through research why certain things were not happening and be there if/when they were corrected. Digging for answers can be both fun and well-rewarding.

⤻

The Banking Corporation (TBC) is illustrative of a special situation that has been fabulous, but has not yet come to complete fruition (see Table 10.2).

During an acquisition of another bank in 1988, TBC issued warrants due to expire 10 years later in November of 1998. A *warrant* is a certificate that gives the holder an option to purchase a number of common shares of a stock at a specified price during a specified period of time. (A warrant is not an option. The difference lies in the expiration dates: Options normally expire in nine months or less, whereas warrants can expire as far in the future as a company desires.)

So, TBC's warrants will expire in November of 1998. The warrants are convertible into TBC common shares at a rate of $62 per share for each warrant owned. If the stock never sells above $62 a share, the warrants will expire valueless in 1998! Risky? Yes. However, if you are familiar with TBC, and know that they have good expectations of earning enough between the present time and 1998 to move the stock, then it seems less of a gamble. I began following this situation years ago, when the warrants were priced at

$3. When the financial sector of the market dropped like a rock in 1989 and 1990, this company's stock plummeted to $16 and the warrants were selling at $1.50. The bank then began restructuring its operations, wrote off losses, and acquired additional banks—thus rebuilding its business. After years of excellent management and an ability to get revenues and earnings on the upswing, the stock in early 1996 is at $100 per share. With this stock price, and with the conversion at $62, the value of the warrants is presently at $38.00!

So, what have you learned here? The stock price has appreciated from $16 to $100 in four years (a percentage gain of 500%). During the same period, the warrants escalated from $1.50 to $38.00 (25 times from its low of $1.50). Incredible, but true. This is called *leverage*. As defined, leverage is the ability to control something large with something smaller. Leverage is utilized as an attempt to get more "bang for the buck." A warrant can be purchased for substantially less than the price of the stock rather than buying the common stock itself. For every $1.00 the stock moves, warrants can move at least $1.00 and possibly more.

The concept of utilizing leverage in the market assumes high risk, but if careful research indicates that the potentials are in your favor, leverage can work as a most powerful tool to make a lot of money—many times more than the stock itself can appreciate.

Table 10.2   Stock and Warrant Prices of TBC

	Stock Price	Conversion	Warrant
1995	$100.00	$62.00	$38.00
1994	$ 65.00	$62.00	$ 3.00
1993	$ 61.00	$62.00	$ 2.00
1992	$ 54.00	$62.00	$ 1.50
1991	$ 36.00	$62.00	$ 1.50

The figures in Table 10.3 bear out the growth rate of TBC and the reasons for the appreciation in its stock price.

Table 10.3   TBC Profile

	Stock Prices			Revs	Net Income	BV/	
	High	Low	EPS	(M)	(M)	SH	Div
1995	$100.00	$57.00	$9.14	$2.72	$5,327	$914	$24.17
1994	$ 66.50	$49.25	$7.84	$2.18	$4,251	$749	$22.34
1993	$ 61.00	$50.50	$5.74	$1.70	$3,822	$559	$20.33
1992	$ 54.00	$30.00	$4.44	$1.52	$3,582	$369	$19.26
1991	$ 36.00	$16.25	$1.28	$1.66	$4,224	$122	$17.92

∽

Another special situation that appears to be evolving to exciting long-term proportions is the Fingerprint Corporation (FC). FC designs, manufactures, and markets a wide range of fingerprint-based identification systems used in the verification of a person's identity. FC's equipment is used in law enforcement, welfare identification, child-care screening, refugee identification, immigration, employee background checks, licensing, time, and attendance. F.C. workstations are presently being used in more than 25 states, not to mention the present installation of 85 workstations in all New York City Police Department precincts as well as supplying scanning systems to the Alameda County and Marin County, California, Sheriff's Departments. They also supply biometric systems to verify time and attendance in Southeast Asia and the Pacific Rim.

What does this all add up to? Let's look at the figures in Table 10.4.

Table 10.4   The Fingerprint Corporation Profile

| | Stock Prices | | | Revs | Net Income | BV/ |
	High	Low	EPS	(M)	(M)	SH
1996★	$19.25	$9.12	.04	$25.8	$.89	——
1995	$16.75	$2.87	-.04	$27.0	- .7	$.49
1994	$ 4.06	$2.31	-.14	$20.1	-2.6	$.19
1993	$ 3.93	$1.50	-.20	$11.9	-3.0	$.04
1992	$ 4.50	$2.00	-.24	$ 3.7	-3.0	——

★ for the nine months from July 1 to March 31, 1996

For the first nine months ending March 31, 1996, FC's revenues were $25.8 million versus $19.7 million during the same period in 1995. Net income from operations also shows great improvement to a profit of $.04 versus a deficit of $.02 during the same period of 1995. Notice that this is a small company in a very young industry that has found its niche—to verify the identity of persons everywhere. Even the FBI by the year 2000 wants to create a paper-less fingerprint database. Biometric devices are estimated to generate approximately $100 million in revenues in 1996, and it is estimated that the market should grow to $1 billion in five years. If FC can maintain an estimated annual growth rate of 35% to 50%, and management can absorb their growing pains and keep their ship on course, it could be a great ride in the next few years.

If your research shows that the growth rate in earnings, along with all the other guidelines, indicate that the odds favor you and not the "house," then go ahead and make your decision.

CHAPTER 11

Exceptions That Prove the Rules

Of course there are exceptions to every rule—and investment rules are no different. You will find exceptions by doing research beyond the numbers. For example, if a company is expanding by opening new stores, outlets, restaurants, or offices, or if it's making new acquisitions within the same industry, it would appear that, with no additional debt (remember—one of my parameters is little or no debt), the company could add increased revenue and earnings growth. If a company continues to split its stock year after year, that's usually a sure indication of increased revenues, earnings, and stock prices. These are two good signs to look out for. It's also a sign of corporate professionalism by top management.

There are times when a company's directors want to conserve their cash but want to reward their share-holders. So they declare a stock dividend or a stock split, which might vary greatly from a 10% stock dividend (1 share of stock for every 10 shares owned) up to 4 or 5 shares for every share owned. How great the split will be depends on the company's board of directors. If a stock sells in the $60 or $70 range, it probably would split 2 for 1, although that would only be a supposition. It could be a 10% stock dividend, or a 2 or 3 for 1 split.

Years ago, a company in the oil industry declared a 10% stock dividend every year for years. Other companies have split their stock 2 for 1 in each of the last four years.

If a company declares a 2 for 1 stock split, it simply means that for every share you own the company will give you another—so you will now have two shares for every one owned previously. When this occurs, the price of the stock will be cut in half; for example, if the stock price is $50 and there is a 2 for 1 stock split, your shares (of which you now have twice as many) will be reduced by half, to $25 per share. In essence, the total value of your shares is the same—100 shares valued at $50 per share is worth as much as 200 shares valued at $25 per share.

The advantage in this, if there is any, is that when earnings drive the stock prices higher, the value of your 200 shares increases $2 for every $1 the stock goes up. If you own 100 shares and the stock goes up $10, you are richer by $1,000. If you own 200 following the split, and the stock increases $10, you are $2,000 richer. Of course, the opposite can occur if the stock splits 2 for 1 and drops $10—you would be $2,000 poorer.

Establish effective guidelines and parameters to purchase growth companies, and you'll be on your way to a potentially profitable experience in the stock market—much the same way as professionals structure their successful strategies for their companies.

Beware of Pitfalls

From my standpoint, there are many pitfalls you face as an investor, and it's important to know about them so that you can be on guard.

First, trying to time the market by buying at the lows and selling at the highs may not be the best strategy and, in my opinion, is a waste of time. No one has consistently succeeded in doing this over the long term. History tells us that the odds are in the favor of those who buy stocks for the long haul. Many ask where stock prices are heading. The answer to that question is simple. On balance, the stock market goes up more than down. One of the major reasons rests with economic growth. The 2.5% growth of the economy in 1995 produced more than $100 billion of goods and services than in 1994, and the beat goes on. Even with slower growth in our economy, to let's say, 1.5%, this powerful nation will still see a $20 to $30 billion increase in goods and services. Steady growth in past decades and in future ones equate to our continued expanding economy, which has been and always will be good for stock prices.

Second, don't be too concerned about whether the stock market is going up or down. If a company is a good one, expect to hold onto it for some time, even though the market becomes volatile. Bull markets (when stocks go higher) have been known to last a long time (possibly years), rising less steeply as compared to market drops. Bear markets (when stocks drop in value) can last for months and drop rapidly, but the stocks whose earnings are continuing to explode on the upside usually withstand market declines the best. For example, according to Ibbotson Associates, Inc., $1 invested in stocks in 1926 grew to $800.08 as of year-end 1993—even with wars and depressions! That's as powerful an endorsement as I can think of—stocks have been a good hedge against inflation and have appreciated over a long time.

Another pitfall to avoid is wishful thinking—the idea that this year will be different from others. Every year is different, but it makes little difference which way the market goes from one year to the next. As long as you own good companies with good management and continued earnings growth, it stands to reason that the stock of these companies should appreciate over time. Conversely, if a company has lower earnings or is cyclical in nature, then the company's stock could be adversely affected by economic conditions.

One of the most important aspects of investing is knowing about the company you're investing in. Even if your broker tells you this is a terrific company (and it may be), be sure to learn as much as you can about the company, its "niche" in its industry's market, its past history, and its potential future growth rate.

Finally, keep in mind that every purchase should be designed to be in your portfolio over the long-term. Leave the speculating and short-term trading to others.

No Free Rides

Now a word about brokers. I'm always seeing ads for "no fee" brokers or reduced commissions. What I don't see are ads proving *results*. If you're serious about investing, results, not saving commission costs, should be your goal. A good broker who uses a sound investment structure can help you make a lot of money and earn his or her commission many times over. Just ask my clients! Keep in mind, also, that over several years of long-term investing, annual commission rates are automatically reduced, simply because you will hold onto stocks longer.

My father taught me that you get what you pay for—and that there are no free rides. This applies, also, to securing the services of a broker who will guide you toward the best returns on your investment— in the short run and the long run as well.

CHAPTER 12

Market Hype, Emotions, and Gut Feelings

W hen you're developing a long-term investment program, keep in mind that
newspapers, magazines, and the financial
channels on television tend to "hype" the financial
news. You will rarely be given more than short-term
information. In other words, one week everybody will
be talking about inflation going higher and interest
rates threatening the market, and the next week about
interest rates falling and inflation finally under control
due to lower oil prices. Brokerage firms put companies
on their "buy" lists or "sell" lists, and market analysts
tout stocks for appreciation. These "trend followers"
use short-term indicators. Remember: Short-term
investing makes money for the broker, but not always
for the investor.

To be brutally honest, there's a built-in conflict of
interest between broker and client. A broker's income

is based on transactions, not on results. The more a broker trades an account, the more money he or she earns. The less the broker trades, the more money the client will make, assuming he or she owns the right stocks.

That's why I stress the long-term—selling only when situations occur that will enable you to upgrade your account by buying stocks with better potential than stocks currently in the portfolio.

Although this may shock some of you, there does come a time when the stocks you own, no matter which stocks you own—yes, even IBM, Xerox, Polaroid, GM, Ford, Wal-Mart, or Home Depot, for example—no longer meet the criteria used to build your portfolio. Eventually the time comes when a company's stock reaches its potential and the risk of owning those stocks increases due to failing earnings or the flattening of the earnings curve. The bottom line is: never fall in love with a stock to the point where you'll hold onto it no matter what! There always comes a time, no matter what the stock is, to say "adios."

What should you expect from your broker? Expect someone who will keep you well-informed about significant corporate changes that could impact the price of the stock. Tell your broker that you want to get earnings reports and all other information you need to make a sensible evaluation of any new potential stock purchases. Whatever your guidelines are, your broker should stick to those guidelines when looking to add to your portfolio or sell off stocks.

Again, fair warning: Be cautious about short-term market hype.

∾

Love, hate, euphoria, fear, anger—all of these emotions find their way into the marketplace at one time or another. Everyone who buys and sells according to a "gut" feeling will experience these roller-coaster rides. People who let emotion creep into their investment decisions are always uneasy because of the short-term fluctuations in the market. If you find this happening to you, take it as a warning to re-evaluate your investment situation. Investors regret decisions based on emotion farther down the road. Believe me.

I used to be the kind of broker who watched the stock market's daily ups and downs. Every day, I used to live or die by the Dow. It was an emotional ride— too emotional. One day, my heart told me to slow down, the hard way. One quadruple bypass later, I changed my tune forever. I changed everything. I started a diet of low-fat foods and quiet, intelligent investment decisions. I looked deeper; I did my homework. And in the end I became a better broker—not only for me but for my clients, too. All because I began using my brain and stopped using my gut as a barometer.

So don't get so worked up. Just use your head and stay cool. Always consider the hard facts before making an investment decision. If you have purchased a stock based on fact, you should not be concerned if the price falls. If the fundamentals remain intact and the stock continues to fall, it just may be the time to elect to buy, not sell. Legendary investors who have always bought shares of good companies have always gone on spending sprees when their stocks were down (enabling them to purchase more shares at lower prices). When you feel panic and are ready to throw in the towel and sell, that is precisely the time to be buying. Purchasing stocks based on facts will make you happier and more successful. A sound investment structure allows you to relax and watch the stock prices in your portfolio be driven by earnings rather than hype.

The important thing to remember is always look at your investments in the long term. Daily or weekly movements in the stock market are not for you. Leave those fluctuations to the short-term investors. Soon enough they'll want to know your secret.

CHAPTER 13

The Whens and Whys of Selling

By far the most difficult task to assess is knowing when and why to sell a stock—has the stock performed poorly or has it appreciated so much in value that you want to get out before the price drops? Sometimes the overall condition of the stock market may be unfavorable for most stocks to appreciate, which may cause dramatic market fluctuations—up one day and down the next. If the market is in one of these cycles, it's virtually impossible to determine whether you should get out of the market. If your stocks are not dramatically impacted by the market swings—just hold on.

Some time ago, I received a call from a 72-year-old woman who told me her tax attorney had referred her to four brokers, and she had to choose one. Her last broker had lost 40% of her assets in six years. After two 2-hour meetings with the woman, I suggested she see the other three brokers. But she didn't go; she told me she wasn't going anywhere else. She had been looking for a broker who would explain in detail the choosing of a portfolio and share the investment decisions with her—and she'd found that in me. Her losses had occurred because her stock purchases were probably not monitored on an ongoing basis; and those losses were possibly due to a change in the growth rate and earnings of the companies in which she'd invested. In other words, she and her broker didn't know when to sell.

Remember, revenues and/or earnings must be analyzed closely on a quarterly basis, or even more frequently, to determine a potential change in the direction of a company's growth. Lack of growth can seriously damage a company's credibility in the market, thereby adversely affecting its stock price.

Bad news and analysts' comments between periods of earnings announcements also can have an effect on stock prices. Just recently, a supposed market guru on a television financial channel rumored a drastic reduction in the revenues of a particular company. Its stock dropped 25% in three days. Even if the rumor is erroneous, its effect still can be destructive and long-lasting.

If a company loses revenues and earnings momentum, then it is time to sell and go somewhere else. Take the time to find those companies that keep out of the public eye simply by quietly grinding out revenue and earnings growth, quarter by quarter, without publicity. Announcements of earnings increases and other factual information can be useful; rumors and publicity are not. And while you're at it, set a downside limit on your stock purchases so that if the stock dips to whatever limit you choose—say 10%, 15%, or 20%—sell it and cut your losses. It's no fun to sell a losing position or positions but if you do sell, at least you will have the proceeds of those sales to invest when opportunity knocks once again.

CHAPTER 14

The Facts of Life

This is the last chapter of the book, but it's the beginning of your opportunity to take advantage of what you have learned. As a stock broker and investment advisor, it is my objective to find potentially good companies, analyze them, and ensure as much as possible that for my clients the rewards outweigh the risks of owning common stocks. The market is always going to be "up" sometimes and "down" at others, but if you plan and structure your portfolio with patience and intelligence, you will increase your odds of success.

Research. That's your most important and valuable tool. Use all the information resources at your fingertips and plan carefully. Together, these should lead you to an investment structure based on specific guidelines and parameters—either yours or mine.

It is a fact of life that a negative or losing situation usually feeds on itself; things often go from bad to worse. If you make a mistake in your stock selection (and you will), get out and go on to another situation. Don't wait for all the bad news to evolve and hope the stock will rebound. You're better off upgrading the portfolio with a new stock than waiting for good news that could turn a bad situation around. If you have to take a loss, don't delay—take it.

By the way, you will seldom be able to find a stock price near its lows if revenues and earnings are growing quarter by quarter. So my suggestion is to buy stocks you like, even if they are near or at their highs (see Chapter 6).

What's a fast, easy indicator of what stocks look good? Ask brokers where they are putting their own money. What stocks are they buying for themselves? When a broker can tell you with confidence that almost every investment he or she recommends to you is in his or her own portfolio, it's an ideal situation. (Although it doesn't ensure that they make money even for themselves.) In other words, if your broker isn't willing to "put his money where his mouth is," then I suggest you find a broker who is.

Two final notes.

1. Do not grant anyone discretion in trading or investing in your account. A discretionary account permits the broker, with the permission of the

client, to buy and sell securities in the client's account. This gives the broker total authority over any securities purchased or sold at whatever price, at whatever timing the broker chooses. Giving discretion is very risky and should be avoided. Make it very clear to your broker that you want to discuss every investment decision before it's made; that you want to take an active part in your effort to make money in the stock market.

2. Do not buy and sell securities on margin. In other words, don't borrow against securities you already own to buy more. Brokerage houses will permit you to use your own portfolio as collateral to invest in additional securities. For example, if you have $100,000 in marginable securities in your account, you can purchase an additional $100,000 of marginable securities in your account. If the stocks appreciate in value, your profits can be substantial, but if the stocks drop in value, your losses can also be substantial. In fact, you may even lose all your collateral and then some. In my opinion, that alone makes it too risky. It is better to play by rules that don't leave you exposed to this kind of loss.

The Little Book of Big Profits was created to help all kinds of people make money. You will increase your odds of making money if you know what kinds of companies and what kinds of stocks you're looking for—that is, if you know what kinds of stocks are more likely to show a return for their investors. Follow the guidelines explained in this book. Talk to your broker. With your broker develop a diversified portfolio that, in the long run, will bring you the kind of profit you got into the game to see.

Good planning and good luck!

Glossary

BALANCE SHEET. The financial statement of a business or institution that lists the assets, debts, and owner's investment as of a specific date.

BEAR MARKET. An extended period of a downturn in prices of securities. It does not necessarily mean all stocks or all industries fall in price.

BETA. A mathematical measure of the sensitivity of rates of return of the portfolio as compared with rates of return on the market as a whole. A high beta over 1 indicates moderate or high price volatility. A beta of 1.5 forecasts a 1.5% change in the return on an asset for every 1% change in the return on the market. A beta of 1 means that the stock price will likely move with the market. But no matter what the beta is, by itself it is not a reason to buy (or not buy) any stock.

BLUE CHIP. A very high-quality investment involving a lower-than-average risk of loss of principal or reduction in income. It generally refers to securities of companies having a long history of sustained earnings and dividend payments.

BOOK VALUE. Common shareholders' equity on a per-share basis. Calculated by subtracting liabilities from assets and dividing the remainder by the number of outstanding shares of stock. The book value is what the stock is worth—regardless of its market price.

BULL MARKET. An extended period of time when prices generally increase in value.

COMMON STOCK. A class of capital stock that has no preference to dividends or any distribution of assets. Common stockholders are the residual owners of a corporation, in that they have a claim to what remains after every other party has been paid.

CONVERSION PRICE. The price per share at which common stock is exchanged for a convertible security (warrant, corporate bond, or option).

CURRENT ASSETS. Cash, or an asset expected to be converted into cash within one year. Assets include cash, marketable securities, accounts receivable, inventories, and prepaid expenses. They tend to add liquidity and safety to a firm's operation.

CURRENT RATIO. A measure of the firm's ability to meet its short-term obligations. It is calculated by dividing current liabilities into current assets. A high ratio usually indicates high liquidity as well as conservative and good management. A 5:1 or 6:1 ratio is excellent; 10:1 or 20:1 is even better. If you find a ratio of anything less than 1:1, then that company has greater liabilities than assets and is therefore not viable as an addition to your portfolio.

CYCLICAL STOCK. Common stock of a firm whose profits are heavily influenced by cyclical changes in general economic activity.

DEFICIT. A negative retained-earnings balance. A deficit is the result of a company's accumulated losses and dividend payments exceeding earnings.

DISCRETIONARY ACCOUNT. A brokerage account in which the customer permits the broker to act on the customer's behalf when buying and selling securities. The broker has discretion as to the choice of securities, prices, and timing, subject to any limitations specified in the agreement. Because a discretionary account can be quite risky, it should be avoided.

DIVERSIFICATION. The acquisition of a group of assets in which returns on the assets are not directly related over time. Proper investment diversification, requiring a sufficient number of different assets, reduces the risk in particular securities.

EARNINGS PER SHARE (EPS). Net income for a given period, divided by the average number of common shares outstanding during that period.

EARNINGS. Income of a business; the term usually refers to after-tax income.

EMERGING GROWTH STOCK. The common stock of a relatively young firm operating in an industry with very good growth prospects. Although such stock offers unusually large returns, it could be risky if the expected growth does not occur.

FINANCIAL RISK. The risk that a firm will be unable to meet its financial obligations. This is primarily a function of the relative amount of debt that the firm uses to finance its assets.

GROWTH STOCK. The stock of a firm is expected to have above-average increases in revenues and earnings. These firms normally retain most earnings for reinvestment and therefore pay a small dividend, if any.

HEDGE AGAINST INFLATION. An investment whose growth outpaces inflation.

INCENTIVE STOCK OPTION. An option permitting an employee to purchase shares of the employer's stock at a predetermined price.

INFLATION. A general increase in the price of goods and services. Unexpected inflation tends to be detrimental to security prices, primarily because it forces interest rates higher.

INTEREST RATE RISK. The risk that interest rates will rise and reduce the market value of an investment and the value of stocks. Long-term fixed income securities, such as bonds and preferred stock, subject their owners to the greatest amount of interest rate risk. Short-term instruments are influenced less by interest rate movements.

INTRINSIC VALUE. The value of a security, such as a warrant. The price of a stock less the conversion price of the warrant equals the intrinsic value of the warrant.

LEVERAGE. The ability to control something larger with something smaller. Leverage is utilized as an attempt to get "more bang for your buck."

LIQUIDITY. When a large portion of one's holdings in cash or assets can be converted into cash quickly.

LOSS OF PURCHASING POWER. When inflation rates increase faster than wages, earnings, as well as the value of investments.

MANAGED ACCOUNT. An investment account managed by a broker or other professional.

MARGIN ACCOUNT. A brokerage account that permits an investor to purchase securities by borrowing the cash value out of securities already held in an account. Usually they offer a lower interest rate on the loan, as well as tax deductions on the interest paid. A margin account gives you leverage and in good markets can enhance your returns; the risk is that in bad markets you could lose most or all of your money.

MARKET RISK. The risk that general market pressures will cause the value of an investment to fluctuate. It may be necessary to liquidate a position (sell) during a down period in the cycle. Market risk is highest for securities with above average volatility (such as common stock), and lowest for stable securities (such as treasury bills). Market risk is of little consequence to a person who purchases securities with the intention of holding them for a long period of time.

NET INCOME. Income after all expenses and taxes have been deducted. It is used to calculate various profitability and stock performance measures, including price/earnings ratio, return on equity, and earnings per share.

PRICE/EARNINGS RATIO. The current price of a stock divided by the current earnings per share of the issuing firm. As a rule, a relatively high P/E ratio is an indication that the firm's earnings are likely to grow or the stock price is likely to fall.

REVENUE. The inflow of assets resulting from the sale of goods and services and earnings from dividends, interest, and rent. It is usually received either as cash or as receivables, which can be turned into cash at a later date (also referred to as SALES of a company).

REVERSE STOCK SPLIT. A proportionate decrease in the shares of stock held by stockholders. For example, a "1 for 3" split results in the stockholder owning one share for every three shares owned before the split. A company usually institutes a reverse split in order to increase the market price of the stock by decreasing the number of shares outstanding. A STOCK SPLIT is exactly the opposite.

RISK. The variability of returns from an investment; the greater the variability, the greater the risk.

SHORT TERM. Designating a gain or loss on the value of an asset that has been held less than a specified period of time.

SPECIAL SITUATION. A currently undervalued stock that can suddenly increase in value because of potentially favorable circumstances. Special situations are quite risky.

STOCK SPLIT. When a corporation reduces the market price of its stock (by splitting its stock) to make the shares more attractive to investors. The share price is reduced proportionally with the percentage of increased outstanding shares.

YIELD. The percentage return on an investment. For example, if a stock is selling at a price of $30.00 and pays a $1.00 dividend, then, the stock yields 3.3%—$1.00 divided by its stock price of $30.00. There are many other types of yields, but the example here is used only for purposes in this book.

WARRANT. A certificate that gives to the holder an option to purchase a number of common shares of a stock at a specific price within a specific period of time. A warrant is not an option. The difference lies in the expiration dates. Options normally expire in nine months or less, whereas warrants can expire as far in the future as a company desires. Companies can also extend expirations of warrants, too.